MONUMENT VALLEY
NAVAJO TRIBAL PARK

A VISUAL
INTERPRETATION

"The SPACE BETWEEN the ROCKS"
by
STEWART AITCHISON

MONUMENT VALLEY

NAVAJO TRIBAL PARK

A VISUAL INTERPRETATION

"The SPACE BETWEEN the ROCKS"
by
STEWART AITCHISON

The "classic" view of Monument Valley—East & West Mittens and Merrick Butte, late afternoon.

FRONT COVER PHOTO: West Mitten, late afternoon.

ISBN O-939365-38-3

Printed in Singapore.
First Edition 1994.

ACKNOWLEDGEMENTS

We would like to take this opportunity to thank the many photographers who made their imagery available to us during the editing of this title. While no single image can effectively replace the actual experience of being there, we believe the visual story told by the images contained in this volume do tell the story of seasonal change and process more effectively than what the visitor would experience while on vacation. On behalf of those who will see this book, we thank you for sharing the fruits of your labors.

DEDICATION

A note about Mae—
While the basic biography presented in this essay is loosely based on an actual resident of Monument Valley, stories from many sources were woven into this tale. I could not have written this essay without the generous help of Susie Yazzie, her daughter Effie Holiday, and Susie's grand-daughter Elvina Holiday. Ahéhee'. I also appreciate the suggestions of Kathy Hooker and my wife, Anne Kramer.—S.A.

SIERRA PRESS, INC.

4988 Gold Leaf Drive, Mariposa, CA 95338

CONTENTS

MONUMENT VALLEY

NAVAJO TRIBAL PARK

"Tsé bíyíntzis gaii"
—"the space between the rocks"— is the name some *Diné* (Navajo) give for what white people call Monument Valley. The landscape of Monument Valley is internationally recognized but intimately known only by those few *Diné* who live there. The rock monuments are icons of a West which exists mostly in celluloid imagination, but they also define one of the most beautiful parts of *Dinétáh*, Navajo Country.

"The Space Between the Rocks"—Monument Valley from Hunts Mesa.

The SPACE BETWEEN the ROCKS

by
Stewart Aitchison

Mae's hands look much younger than her years. A lifetime of working with lanolin-rich wool has kept them soft. A finger on each hand is ringed with silver and turquoise the color of the sky. With her left hand, she deftly plucks the woolen warp and slides in a batten, fashioned of hard oak but grooved along the edges by countless days of weaving. The weft dances across the warp like sheep gamboling through the sage. The pattern is spun from her history, trails of her memory. It is the pattern of life.

Outside her *hooghan*, or traditional clay-covered log house, a sheep's bell tinkles softly. The flock works its way across a sandy dune, nibbling Indian rice grass and galleta grass.

Seventy-something springs ago, Mae was born in a *hooghan* nestled against a mesa in the heart of the valley. As a baby, she was placed in a cradleboard, the first of four that would be made for her as she grew. Her mother, a woman of the *Tó dichíí níí* (Bitterwater) Clan, buried the newborn's umbilical cord

In a remote part of Monument Valley, a *Diné* woman sits in front of her upright loom. Her long, graying hair has been carefully combed with a *bé'ézhóó'*, or grass brush, and tied into an hourglass shaped knot in back as instructed by the holy ones. Her name is Mae. She wears a long full skirt of pink cotton that complements her maroon velveteen blouse.

under a nearby pinyon tree to affirm the child's attachment to the land.

Outside the *hooghan*, in the shadow of the towering mesa, grew several netleaf hackberry trees. They, too, were renewing life, sprouting new leaves and blossoming in tiny greenish flowers. The hackberry survives in this harsh land by receiving the benefit of gentle

Old hooghan atop Hunts Mesa.

winter "female" rains that soak into the sand and emerge at the base of the mesa. The tree's berries are relished by birds and rodents, as well as the *Diné*.

Like the sturdy hackberry, the young girl's roots run deep in the shadow of the great mesa, her spirit nourished by the desert's ethereal light, the valley's palpable silence, and vistas that stretch to the edge of the earth. Her playmates will mostly be siblings; neighbors are few and live far away. She will mark her life by the passing of the seasons.

Another spring and her family uses a wooden stick to plant corn in a swale where runoff will supplement the meager rainfall. After harvest, most of the corn will be dried in the sun for later use, but some of the fresh kernels will be scraped off the cob and ground into a soft mush. A little salt may be added and the mixture patted into small cakes, wrapped with the corn husk, and then baked slowly in a pit. For a special occasion, a sheep will be butchered for mutton stew. As the child grows, she becomes especially fond of mush made from blue corn meal obtained from the Hopi people to the south.

After about six winters, trader Harry Goulding starts to bring a few tourists to her family's camp. At first Mae fears the strangers, but as the years pass she becomes fascinated by their unfamiliar language and odd customs. In the coolness of the *chaha' oh*, or summer shade house, Mae's mother would drop round, flat pieces of soft dough into a pan of hot grease to make *dah díníílghaazh*, fry bread, for the visitors.

Mae's mother begins to teach her the secrets of weaving a rug—how to card the wool and spin it into yarn, where to collect the plants for dyeing, and how to construct the loom. Mae's first rugs were small, uneven, simple straight lines of colored weft. But practice brought improvement until eventually she became a fine weaver. The tree-of-life design was repeated endless times, but one day she tried a rug of *yéi* figures, holy beings, and found it wonderful.

Late summer. Clouds build, their bottoms tinted pink from reflected light off the red sand and rock. Lightning lashes the ground, thunder roars through the valley, cloud bellies shred into violent showers. But the storm passes, the clouds part, and yellow beams of sunlight dance across the wet slickrock. The scent of sage is heavy in the air.

Summer, or "male", rains can unleash deadly flash floods, but they can also bring life. Mae cautiously climbs weathered hand-and-toe-holds carved into the soft sandstone a thousand years ago. The

The Mittens & Merrick Butte from the raven's viewpoint.

precarious steps zig and zag up a steep slope to a narrow ledge that angles upward to the mesa top. Several large potholes have eroded out of the flat summit and are brimming with sweet water. Within days, the warm sun will encourage a teeming brew of life in these potholes. Using a tin cup, Mae dips into a pool and pours the precious fluid into a woven jug waterproofed with pinyon pitch. Scarce water. Tenacious life.

The sheep are thirsty. Mae herds the flock around the east side of Thunderbird Mesa, past the bare juniper bones of an abandoned *tá chééh*, or sweat lodge, to the place where a thread of alkaline but palatable water emerges from the foot of an immense golden sand dune. As she moves across the sand, the folds of her voluminous skirt mimic the ripples of the dune. Her red velveteen blouse rivals the color of the sandstone.

The watering place, called Sand Springs, is the only permanent source of water in the valley, but its existence is tenuous. An equilibrium exists between the dune sand being slowly blown across the wash and burying the spring and the scouring action of flash floods. Balance. Harmony.

While the sheep drink their fill, Mae gazes across the bright space of desert and remembers stories told only in winter. Stories of the creation of *Dinétáh*; sagas about the hero twins and their battles at nearby Comb Ridge and the San Juan River;

lessons from Changing Woman who created the people of the earth; Navajo warriors frozen as stone monoliths.

She recalls in Valley of the Gods a trapezoidal block of sandstone on a ridge—it is a stone forked-stick *hooghan* where children disobedient to *Jóhonaàéí* (Sun Bearer) are eternally trapped. And she thinks of the meandering goosenecks of the San Juan River, the coils of a huge serpent, The One Who Crawls With Her Body.

Another story explains how all of Monument Valley is a giant *hooghan*. A butte near Goulding's Trading Post is the *hooghan's* fireplace, the east-facing door is near the Tribal Park ranger station, Sentinel Mesa and Gray Whiskers Mesa are the doorposts.

Many of the large monuments, particularly the Mittens with their spouts, are water barrels. The Mittens are also seen as hands left behind by the gods as signs that one day the holy beings will return and rule from Monument Valley.

Eagle Mesa is an especially sacred place, where the spirit of a dead person goes after burial. One can hear the voices of babies and adults in this area and can see their bones and footprints on the mesa. The tops of all the mesas that align between Douglas Mesa and the Bears Ears—on Elk Ridge near Natural Bridges National Monument—

Bighorn sheep petroglyph & the Sun's Eye arch.

form a pathway walked by the holy beings during their travels.

The monument called Totem Pole and neighboring spires are said to be a line of prayersticks or petrified *yé'ii* held up by lightning. Because people have climbed on the monolith, the spirit is offended and has reduced the amount of rainfall the valley once enjoyed. Many other monoliths of Monument Valley are also holy people frozen in form.

At the northern and southern extremes of the Monument Valley area are igneous rocks—basalt necks or cores—that once fed volcanoes long since eroded away. The *Diné* consider Alhambra Rock to the north to be both a sky supporter as well as a group of holy beings performing a *yé'ii bichei* dance. To the south, El Capitan, or *Agathla*, also supports the sky and is said to transmit information to the sun or to White Shell Woman who lives near the ocean. To the west sits Owl, wife of Big Snake who lives nearby.

There have also been warnings. Behind Goulding's Trading Post is a cliff holding a large white rock. When the rock falls, something bad will happen, an illness, a natural calamity or the death of an important person. When Chaistla Butte near Kayenta tumbles, the world will end.

At night Mae hears Coyote howl. Is the trickster telling the story of how he came across Black God, First Man, and First Woman carefully placing the stars into fixed patterns in the sky? Coyote grabbed the blanket holding the remaining stars and flung the stars upward creating the Milky Way. Skinwalkers, witches, travel between caves on Black Mesa north to the San Juan River. Danger lurks in the darkness.

Another time Mae takes the flock near the Sun's Eye, a huge arch eroded in the ceiling of a towering overhang. Rain water sends an ephemeral waterfall rushing through the opening. Below, mud cracks dissolve into wet, slippery clay. She fashions a toy animal from the clay and pretends it is a wild sheep running across the boulders.

Behind her, against the base of the mesa, are low crumbling walls built a millenium ago by people other than the *Diné*. On the rocks above the ruin are petroglyphs, drawings of horned beasts, perhaps bighorn sheep. Their mouths are open. Long thin horns sweep back in curves over half-moon shaped bodies. Their cloven hooves are obvious. Their bodies are stippled, the result of the artist striking a stone against the black desert varnish that coats the sandstone. The largest of the three figures appears to be jumping over the smallest one. All have erect tails. Is this a record of fleeing animals, are the figures some sort of hunting magic,

Blowing sand beneath Agathla Peak.

they simple doodling? Some *Diné* believe that the ancient rock art panels describe problems and trials of the ancient ones before they were destroyed or moved from the area.

The *Diné* refer to these people as the Anasazi, more correctly spelled 'anaas*ází,* literally "ancestral enemies," referring not only to the ancestors of the pueblo-dwelling people of the Four Corners but also the town-dwelling, pottery-making cultures of central and southern Arizona and New Mexico. The *Diné* perception of the Anasazi tells much more about the *Diné's* world view than it does about these ancient people.

The *Diné* say they met the Anasazi long before this world was created. The two cultures have passed through a number of previous worlds into this present one. The path of white that cuts across the bands of color in the traditional Navajo wedding basket is a reminder of their emergence into this world. For many generations the

Diné and Anasazi peacefully coexisted. The *Diné* were given seeds of corn and pumpkin and taught to farm. Unfortunately, the Anasazi's extensive world knowledge eventually led to a haughty, uncontrolled pride. They placed sacred designs on their finely crafted pottery and baskets. They invented tools that allowed them to plant larger fields and reap bigger harvests. Their population increased in size but

decreased in respect for the sacred. The holy beings started to withhold the rain. Huge winds with swirling fireballs swept through the canyons and killed the people. The black streaks of desert varnish which cover the cliffs and rocks are from the smoke and fire of this destruction.

After the Anasazi left, the *Diné* pondered the empty homes and scattered artifacts. From these objects they learned lessons about proper behavior and how to live a harmonious daily life.

One day, when Mae was about eighteen years old, many white men came to the valley to make a film. This would be the first of many John Wayne westerns shot here, and locals would be hired as extras. In one movie, *Diné* men were filmed as marauding Indians, then they were clothed in cavalry uniforms to play that role as well. This was amusing, but Mae remembered her great-great-grandmother who had perished on the tragic Long Walk to Fort Sumner in New Mexico, and her great-grandmother who had escaped from that prison camp and returned to the valley.

Several years later, a time came to have a sing. More than a thousand people arrived on horseback or in wagons from all corners of *Dinétáh* to a water hole between the Mittens. For three days and three nights

Anasazi ruin in Mystery Valley.

chanting and drum beats filled the desert air. A healing Mud Dance was performed to cure those who were ill, as well as a Squaw Dance to make new friends.

Unfortunately many of the old ways began to fade away. By 1950, Mae's family bought their first *chidí*, or truck, now partially buried in a sand dune. Her four sons and one daughter went to school. Some of her grandchildren are entering college. And though certain modern conveniences have made life easier, Mae still prefers to live near the mesa where she was born. Her sheep still graze the valley. In the morning as darkness begins to fade, Mae greets the sun. For the traditional *Diné*, it is important to be awake then. Supernatural beings come from the east to the *hooghan* to bless it. "If I am awake, they would say that I am their child and bless me with hard goods, livestock, and knowledge. But if I am asleep, hardship and illness would befall me."

The inner conflict to achieve balance between cultures is increasing in today's world. Will the new generations of *Diné* "sleep" through the lessons of their elders? Or will they be able to follow a path of beauty over a landscape that has meaning and the power to teach and protect?

Strangers come with other stories about Monument Valley. Archaeologists say the Anasazi became the modern Pueblo people, and the Navajo are relatively recent arrivals in the Southwest. Geologists maintain that Monument Valley is the result of erosion acting upon massive layers of relatively hard sandstone overlying softer layers of claystone. Unfathomable amounts of time pass and the stone layers are reduced from plateaus to mesas to buttes then finally to dust.

Whose stories are true? One medicine man has said, "That is how you were taught; then it is correct." There is no ultimate, specific truth or way of understanding, but rather room for thought and meditation. Monument Valley inspires both native residents and passing visitors. It can teach us, as the *Diné* say, to walk in beauty.

Her life is intertwined with the landscape the way the yarns on her loom interlace to become a beautiful rug. To the *Diné* the land is not an inanimate mass of earth and rock but a keeper of mystical and spiritual powers. Though water, wood, and minerals are gifts from the land, they are subordinate to the idea that the *Diné* works through nature in establishing relationships.

Monument Valley seen from Hunts Mesa, afternoon.

MONUMENT VALLEY

NAVAJO
TRIBAL PARK

A VISUAL
INTERPRETATION

Yucca beneath fog-shrouded Three Sisters.

Sunrise, The Mittens & Merrick Butte from the Visitor Center.   16

Melting snow on a wet sand dune near Sand Spring.

The Totem Pole & sand dune, clearing winter storm.

Merrick Butte & Sentinel Mesa shrouded in morning fog.

Frozen waterfall in Narrow Canyon.

Totem Pole and sand dune on a windy Spring morning.

Teardrop Arch, near Goulding's Trading Post.

West Mitten and rainbow.

Crumbling cliff of deChelly Sandstone.

Virga & Monument Valley from Muley Point, Utah.

Towers, monuments & buttes seen from North Window.

The Three Sisters.

Jimson weed (sacred datura) and sandstone wall.   28

Handprint pictographs in Mystery Valley.

West Mitten glowing in the light of sunset.

Seen from near its base, West Mitten is framed by a Utah juniper.

Sand dune & moon.

Totem Pole and Yeii Bichei Rocks with thunderheads, dusk.

Square House Ruin (Anasazi).

34

The view of Monument Valley from Hunts Mesa.

Flashflood near the base of Mitchell Mesa.

Horses grazing near Sentinel Mesa.

The Mittens & Merrick Butte, sunset.

Abandoned firepit in Anasazi ruin.

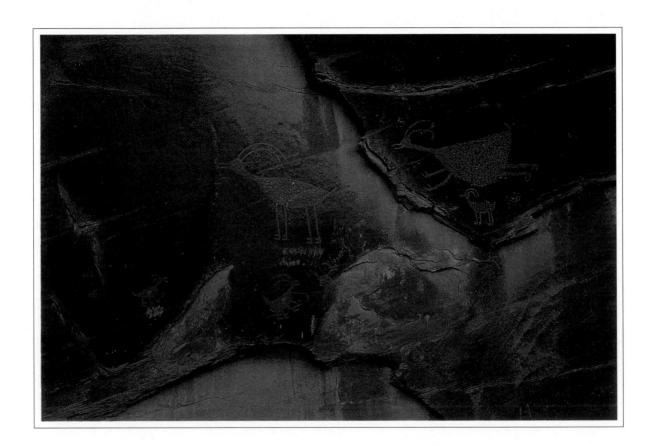

Bighorn sheep petroglyphs at The Sun's Eye.   40

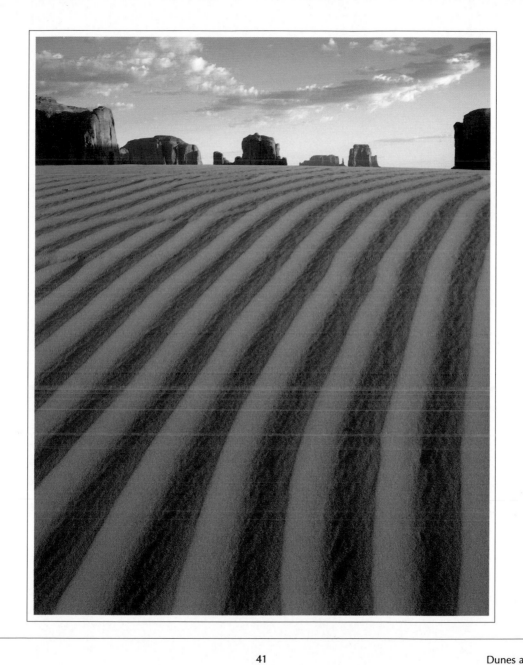

Dunes and distant monoliths.

Sandstone spire in Valley of the Gods.

The glow of sunset seen from Hunts Mesa.

Monuments seen from near Goulding's Trading Post.

Monument Valley seen from Muley Point, Utah.

The Mittens at sunrise.

SUGGESTED READING

Abbey, Edward. *Desert Solitaire: A Season in the Wilderness.* New York, NY: Simon and Schuster. 1968.

Aitchison, Stewart. *A Traveler's Guide to Monument Valley.* Stillwater, MN: Voyageur Press, Inc. 1993.

Hooker, Kathy Eckles. *Time Among the Navajo: Traditional Lifeways on the Reservation.* Santa Fe, NM: Museum of New Mexico Press. 1991.

Lister, Florence C. and Robert H. Lister. *Those Who Came Before.* Tucson, AZ: Southwest Parks and Monuments Association. 1989.

Lister, Florence C. *Windows of the Past: The Ruins of the Southwest.* El Portal, CA: Sierra Press, Inc. 1993.

Locke, Raymond. *The Book of the Navajo.* Los Angeles, CA: Mankind Publishing Co. 1992.

Markwood, Anne. *Monument Valley Navajo Tribal Park.* Santa Barbara, CA: Companion Press. 1992.

Moon, Samuel. *Tall Sheep: Harry Goulding, Monument Valley Trader.* Norman, OK: Univerlity of Oklahoma Press. 1992.

Ortiz, Alfonso, editor. *Handbook of the North American Indians, Volume 10.* Washington, D.C.: Smithsonian Institution. 1979.

In addition—Tony Hillerman has written numerous mystery novels set on the Navajo Reservation that give wonderful insights into contemporary Navajo life.—S.A.

Both the Visitor Center at Monument Valley Navajo Tribal Park as well as the Gift Shop at Goulding's Lodge have many excellent titles available for sale. For further information contact:

Visitor Center Gift Shop
PO Box 360289
Monument Valley, UT 84536
(801) 727-3287

Goulding's Lodge Gift Shop
PO Box 1
Monument Valley, UT 84536
(801) 727-3231

PHOTOGRAPHIC CREDITS

Frank Balthis: Back Cover (left).
Barbara A. Brundege: 12,34,39.
Michael Collier: 9.
Charles Cramer: 43.
Dick Dietrich: 46.
Jack W. Dykinga: 15,19,21.
Jeff Francis: 17,18,20,28,35,38.
Kerrick James: 13,23,Back Cover (right).
Gary Ladd: 26,30,44.
William Neill: 24,32.
Kurt Rhody: 37,45.
Randall K. Roberts: 40.
Barbara Rowell (Mountain Light): Front Cover.
Galen Rowell (Mountain Light): 27.
Jim Stimson: 25.
Tom Till: 2,3,7,8,10,11,16,22,29,31,33,36,41.
Barbara Von Hoffman: Back Cover (middle).
John Ward: 42.

CREDITS

"The Space Between the Rocks" by Stewart Aitchison.
Monument Valley Map by Jeff Nicholas.
Edited by Rose Houk.
Book Design by Jeff Nicholas.
Photo Editor: Jeff Nicholas.
Printing coordinated by TWP, Ltd., Berkeley, Ca.
Printed in Singapore, 1994.

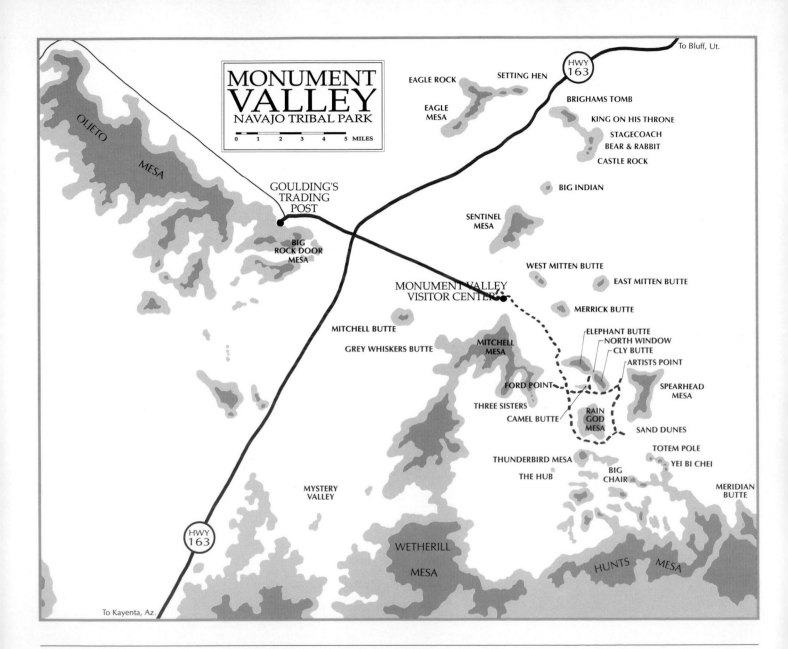

MONUMENT VALLEY
NAVAJO TRIBAL PARK

0 1 2 3 4 5 MILES

OLJETO MESA

To Bluff, Ut.

HWY 163

EAGLE ROCK

SETTING HEN

EAGLE MESA

BRIGHAMS TOMB

KING ON HIS THRONE

STAGECOACH

BEAR & RABBIT

CASTLE ROCK

BIG INDIAN

SENTINEL MESA

GOULDING'S TRADING POST

BIG ROCK DOOR MESA

WEST MITTEN BUTTE

EAST MITTEN BUTTE

MONUMENT VALLEY VISITOR CENTER

MERRICK BUTTE

MITCHELL BUTTE

GREY WHISKERS BUTTE

MITCHELL MESA

ELEPHANT BUTTE

NORTH WINDOW

CLY BUTTE

ARTISTS POINT

FORD POINT

SPEARHEAD MESA

THREE SISTERS

CAMEL BUTTE

RAIN GOD MESA

SAND DUNES

TOTEM POLE

THUNDERBIRD MESA

YEI BI CHEI

THE HUB

BIG CHAIR

MERIDIAN BUTTE

MYSTERY VALLEY

HWY 163

WETHERILL MESA

HUNTS MESA

To Kayenta, Az.